M. Lukic

MW01709772

Grades 3-5

CONTEMPORARY CLOZE

Written by George Moore

Published with the permission of R.I.C. Publications Pty. Ltd.

First published by R.I.C. Publications Pty. Ltd., Perth, Western Australia. Revised by Didax Educational Resources.

Printed in the United States of America.

Order Number 2-5237
ISBN 1-58324-201-5

A B C D E F 09 08 07 06 05

Didax
Educational Resources

395 Main Street
Rowley, MA 01969
www.worldteacherspress.com

Foreword

Cloze *is an effective teaching strategy widely used to assist in the development of reading and comprehension skills. Students develop semantic and syntactic skills as they use the context clues around the missing words in the text to make sense of each individual sentence.*

As the title suggests, Contemporary Cloze – Grades 3 to 5 *covers a wide range of contemporary topics. These include up-to-date information about popular interests or themes, recent inventions or developments, and discussion about a selection of contemporary issues.*

A variety of learning areas is covered including science, society and environment, technology, the arts, health, and physical education.

Other titles in this series: Contemporary Cloze – Grades 1 to 3
Contemporary Cloze – Grades 6 to 8

The author wishes to thank his wife, Mary Moore, for her assistance during the writing of this book.

Contents

Teacher's Notes

Contemporary Cloze provides students with the opportunity to practice using semantic and syntactic skills to assist in the development of reading and comprehension. Students use the context clues around the missing words in the text to make sense of individual sentences.

A variety of contemporary topics is covered including popular student interests or themes, recent inventions or developments, and discussions about contemporary issues.

In some activities, students are provided with the list of missing words. After reading the text, students should sort out the obvious choices first and cross out the words as they are used.

Sometimes students will need to refer to a map, diagram, or illustration to work out the missing word.

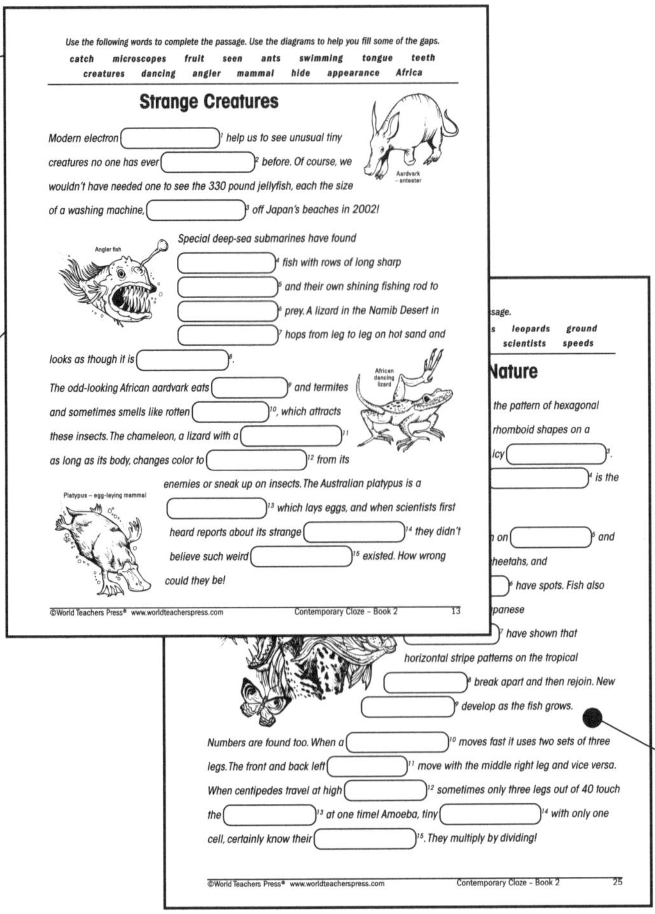

Use the following words to complete the passage. Use the diagrams to help you fill some of the gaps.

catch microscopes fruit seen ants swimming tongue teeth creatures dancing angler mammal hide appearance Africa

Strange Creatures

Modern electron ______[1] help us to see unusual tiny creatures no one has ever ______[2] before. Of course, we wouldn't have needed one to see the 330 pound jellyfish, each the size of a washing machine, ______[3] off Japan's beaches in 2002!

Special deep-sea submarines have found ______[4] fish with rows of long sharp ______[5] and their own shining fishing rod to ______[6] prey. A lizard in the Namib Desert in ______[7] hops from leg to leg on hot sand and looks as though it is ______[8].

The odd-looking African aardvark eats ______[9] and termites and sometimes smells like rotten ______[10], which attracts these insects. The chameleon, a lizard with a ______[11] as long as its body, changes color to ______[12] from its enemies or sneak up on insects. The Australian platypus is a ______[13] which lays eggs, and when scientists first heard reports about its strange ______[14] they didn't believe such weird ______[15] existed. How wrong could they be!

...sage.

...s leopards ground scientists speeds

...Nature

... the pattern of hexagonal ... rhomboid shapes on a ... icy ______. ... ______[4] is the ... on ______[5] and ... heetahs, and ... ______[6] have spots. Fish also ... panese ... ______[7] have shown that horizontal stripe patterns on the tropical ______[8] break apart and then rejoin. New ______[9] develop as the fish grows.

Numbers are found too. When a ______[10] moves fast it uses two sets of three legs. The front and back left ______[11] move with the middle right leg and vice versa. When centipedes travel at high ______[12] sometimes only three legs out of 40 touch the ______[13] at one time! Amoeba, tiny ______[14] with only one cell, certainly know their ______[15]. They multiply by dividing!

The missing words may be a random selection or a specific group of words such as nouns, verbs, or adjectives.

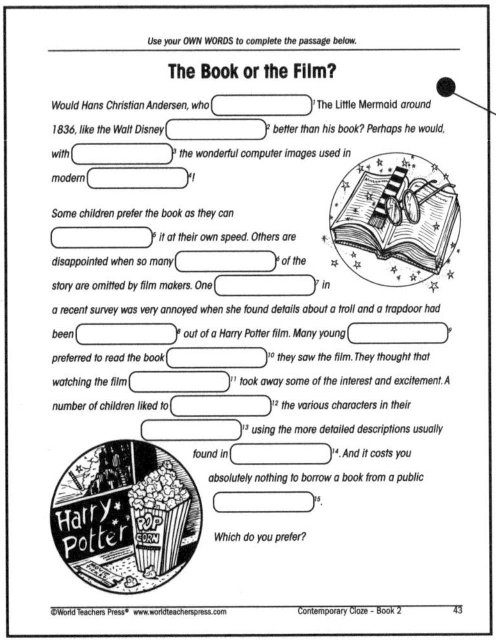

Use your OWN WORDS to complete the passage below.

The Book or the Film?

Would Hans Christian Andersen, who ______[1] The Little Mermaid around 1836, like the Walt Disney ______[2] better than his book? Perhaps he would, with ______[3] the wonderful computer images used in modern ______[4]!

Some children prefer the book as they can ______[5] it at their own speed. Others are disappointed when so many ______[6] of the story are omitted by film makers. One ______[7] in a recent survey was very annoyed when she found details about a troll and a trapdoor had been ______[8] out of a Harry Potter film. Many young ______[9] preferred to read the book ______[10] they saw the film. They thought that watching the film ______[11] took away some of the interest and excitement. A number of children liked to ______[12] the various characters in their ______[13] using the more detailed descriptions usually found in ______[14]. And it costs you absolutely nothing to borrow a book from a public ______[15].

Which do you prefer?

In other activities, students must choose their own words to complete the text. Again, students should sort out the obvious choices first. Students may choose words different from the answers provided. These may still be correct if used in the proper context.

Teacher's Notes

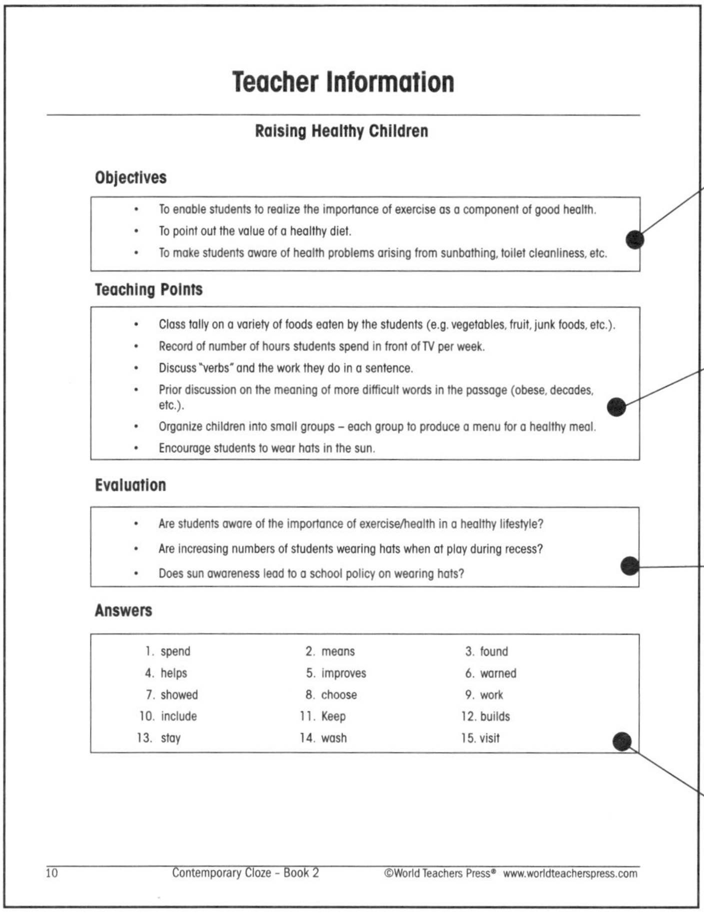

Teacher Information

Raising Healthy Children

Objectives

- To enable students to realize the importance of exercise as a component of good health.
- To point out the value of a healthy diet.
- To make students aware of health problems arising from sunbathing, toilet cleanliness, etc.

Teaching Points

- Class tally on a variety of foods eaten by the students (e.g. vegetables, fruit, junk foods, etc.).
- Record of number of hours students spend in front of TV per week.
- Discuss "verbs" and the work they do in a sentence.
- Prior discussion on the meaning of more difficult words in the passage (obese, decades, etc.).
- Organize children into small groups – each group to produce a menu for a healthy meal.
- Encourage students to wear hats in the sun.

Evaluation

- Are students aware of the importance of exercise/health in a healthy lifestyle?
- Are increasing numbers of students wearing hats when at play during recess?
- Does sun awareness lead to a school policy on wearing hats?

Answers

1. spend	2. means	3. found
4. helps	5. improves	6. warned
7. showed	8. choose	9. work
10. include	11. Keep	12. builds
13. stay	14. wash	15. visit

10 Contemporary Cloze - Book 2 ©World Teachers Press® www.worldteacherspress.com

Objectives for each topic are included.

Teaching points provide discussion points, additional activities and terms which may need explanation.

A number of evaluation points allow teachers to assess the success or failure of a lesson.

Answers are included for all worksheet activites.

Further suggestions:

- The topic can be discussed with the whole class or in small groups before students complete the cloze activity.
- Some of the contemporary topics suggest further discussion following the completion of the activity. Reports by small research groups on particular topics could feature in a series of lessons.
- Unless you want to assess the ability of individual students, the cloze activities could be completed in pairs to enable an interchange of ideas. This works well with less capable readers, who could be partnered with a reader of the same ability or learn from a more capable student.
- Encourage the use of dictionaries to clarify the meaning of difficult words.
- You could review with the students a particular part of speech for the activities where a specific group of words is missing. These include:

  Nouns are naming words like "dog," "Africa," "summer."

  Adjectives are words which describe nouns or words which represent nouns (pronouns). Adjectives usually appear in front of the word they describe but can appear after that word: e.g. "The boy is tall."

  Verbs used are mainly "action" words; e.g. "run," "fly," "skate," etc.

Teacher's Notes

Relevant background information has been included where necessary for each topic.

Graffiti .... **Page 18 – 19**

- In the early days, graffiti was mainly used by street gangs and political activists wanting to get their messages to the public.

Dinosaurs .... **Page 20 – 21**

- A person who is an expert on prehistoric life through the study of fossils is a paleontologist.

Patterns and Numbers in Nature .... **Page 24 – 25**

- A growing amoeba divides into a pair of smaller cells, each one a new amoeba. So amoebas multiply by dividing!

Games Around the World .... **Page 28 – 29**

- The class could be split into small groups to play the games listed. They could then rotate round the games during the lesson(s).
- Haba Gaba: African children may have used nuts, rocks, etc., but beanbags or rolled-up socks can be used.

Nature Fights Back .... **Page 32 – 33**

- Fire ants in America and Australia are believed to have been imported accidentally in ships' cargoes.

Our Changing Language .... **Page 36 – 37**

- See how many shortened words the class can find—a group competition?

Benefits from Space Research .... **Page 40 – 41**

- The infrared sensors react to the heat given off by objects like pottery, which stand out as three-dimensional images.
- Shuttles have to withstand high temperatures (up to 2900°F) caused by friction as they re-enter the Earth's atmosphere.
- NASA – National Aeronautics and Space Administration.

The Water Cycle .... **Page 46 – 47**

- When air cools it contracts. This brings water droplets in clouds closer together to form larger drops as they touch. These larger drops are heavier and can't be held up by the air currents in clouds so they fall as rain.
- Wet a patch on the blackboard. Wait for a while and it disappears, which shows evaporation has occurred.

The Harry Potter Phenomenon .... **Page 50 – 51**

- *The Little White Horse* was written by Elizabeth Goudge and was the Carnegie Medal-winning book in 1946.

Astronauts .... **Page 54 – 55**

- Radiation storms are bursts of electrically charged cosmic rays which travel through space at almost the speed of light. The radiation belts around Jupiter are much stronger than those around Earth and pose a threat to any space exploration.
- Gravity: Microgravity is a greatly reduced pull of gravity, whereas zero gravity is weightlessness in space.

Teacher Information

Bicycles! Bicycles! Bicycles!

Objectives

- To develop reading skills using a familiar and interesting topic.
- To reinforce the skill of gaining information from graphs.
- To underline the value of bicycles as a means of transportation in densely populated countries.
- To familiarize students with the layout of a letter.

Teaching Points

- Discuss the importance of the bicycle to both children and adults, esp. in China and India.
- Debate: "It would be better if we all used bicycles rather than cars." (less pollution, fewer road deaths, etc.)
- Use atlases to locate the countries and cities mentioned.
- Class to bring different types of bikes to school to give talks and discuss: good safety maintenance, road sense etc.
- Students on vacation – send a similar letter to class.
- The popularity of bicycles in a flat country like Holland.

Evaluation

- Were students able to glean information from the graph?
- Did students realize the importance of the bicycle to ordinary families in countries like China and India (e.g. wedding gift)?
- Are students aware of the dangers of riding to school on busy roads?
- Were there positive results from the student bicycle talks (active discussion, sensible points raised, etc.)?

Answers

1. vacation	2. three	3. America
4. Japan	5. popular	6. gifts
7. school	8. accidents	9. crowded
10. roads	11. barriers	12. cars
13. factories	14. year	15. copied

Use the following words to complete the letter. You will need to read the graph to fill some of the spaces.

accidents Japan school copied gifts America roads year crowded vacation cars popular factories barriers three

---

Bicycles! Bicycles! Bicycles!

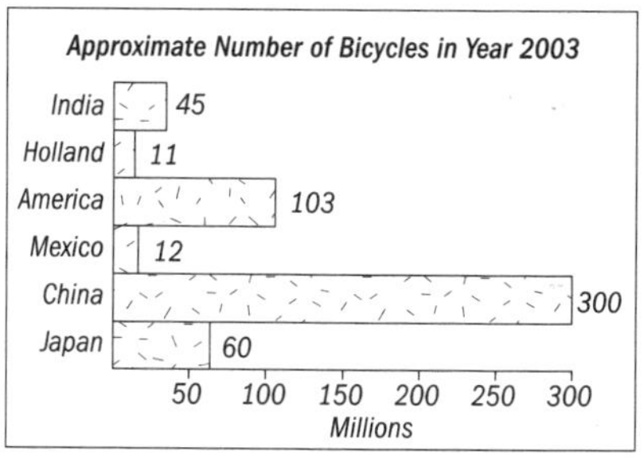

Guilin Cottages,

March 5

Dear Roslyn,

I'm enjoying our ________[1] traveling around China but I've never seen so many bicycles! This country has ________[2] hundred million, about three times the number in ________[3] and five times as many as ________[4]. I bet when bikes were invented over 150 years ago they didn't realize they would be so ________[5]. In China, a bicycle has usually been one of the wedding ________[6] a groom gives his bride!

Bicycles are used for local travel such as going to ________[7] or to work. Millions jam the streets of cities and many cyclists die in road ________[8] because they swerve in and out of traffic. To encourage people to use old, ________[9] public buses, Beijing, China's capital, has banned bikes from busy ________[10] between 7:00 a.m. and 8:00 a.m. They're also removing protective ________[11] or trees which separate car lanes from bicycles. Guangzhou has banned ________[12] over 15 years old and motorcycles from its city center. That means more bikes!

Next week we go to Shanghai where ________[13] produce over four million bicycles every ________[14]. Let's hope there's a subway!

Your friend, Jane.

P.S. I ________[15] the graph from a magazine.

Teacher Information

Raising Healthy Children

Objectives

- To enable students to realize the importance of exercise as a component of good health.
- To point out the value of a healthy diet.
- To make students aware of health problems arising from sunbathing, toilet cleanliness, etc.

Teaching Points

- Class tally on a variety of foods eaten by the students (e.g. vegetables, fruit, junk foods, etc.).
- Record of number of hours students spend in front of TV per week.
- Discuss "verbs" and the work they do in a sentence.
- Prior discussion on the meaning of more difficult words in the passage (obese, decades, etc.).
- Organize children into small groups – each group to produce a menu for a healthy meal.
- Encourage students to wear hats in the sun.

Evaluation

- Are students aware of the importance of exercise/health in a healthy lifestyle?
- Are increasing numbers of students wearing hats when at play during recess?
- Does sun awareness lead to a school policy on wearing hats?

Answers

1. spend	2. means	3. found
4. helps	5. improves	6. warned
7. showed	8. choose	9. work
10. include	11. Keep	12. builds
13. stay	14. wash	15. visit

Use the following VERBS to complete the passage.

Keep warned means choose wash showed improves spend found include helps work visit builds stay

Raising Healthy Children

Many children in developed countries ______ 1 too much time in front of TV or computer screens. The drop in physical exercise ______ 2 20% of American children are obese, one of the highest rates ______ 3 in developed nations! Regular exercise is important as it ______ 4 to prevent weight problems and ______ 5 the work done by the heart and lungs.

For decades, American doctors have ______ 6 parents about high levels of fat and sugar in "junk" foods. Research in 2002 ______ 7 Americans still spend around $200 billion on fast food each year, with over 300 companies to ______ 8 from! The high fat content in "junk" foods means the body has to ______ 9 much harder to digest it. A child's diet should ______ 10 plenty of vegetables, cereals, and fruit. ______ 11 french fries, cakes, icecream, etc. for special occasions. Your body constantly ______ 12 new cells so your skin, brain, muscles, and bones come from the same source—food.

As well as diet and exercise, there are some other simple steps to ______ 13 healthy. Don't carry heavy school bags, which can lead to neck and back problems, take care in the sun and always ______ 14 your hands after you ______ 15 the toilet. Good health is so important as you grow up.

Teacher Information

Strange Creatures

Objectives

- To develop reading skills using a cloze passage on a topic interesting to children.
- To give students practice in gleaning information from illustrations to complete gaps in the passage.
- To inform students about the strange creatures that inhabit our world.

Teaching Points

- How these creatures have developed adaptations to exist in a variety of habitats.
- Encourage the use of atlases to locate the regions noted in the passage.
- Organize brief oral reports by the students – "My Strange Creature" following library or Internet research.
- Following research or discussion by the teacher, students color in the diagrams in appropriate colors.
- Discuss pronunciation/meanings of the more difficult words.
- Record on a blank world map (wall map or student map) the locations of each animal from "My Strange Creature" student talks.
- Children to draw or paint their own "strange creature" plus a short explanation of its strangest feature.

Evaluation

- How well did the students glean necessary information from the illustrations?
- Did the students research well/enjoy the information for their talks?
- Do students appreciate that all creatures, unusual or not, deserve their place in the world?
- Were results more favorable on a topic that is interesting to young children?

Answers

1. microscopes	2. seen	3. swimming
4. angler	5. teeth	6. catch
7. Africa	8. dancing	9. ants
10. fruit	11. tongue	12. hide
13. mammal	14. appearance	15. creatures

Use the following words to complete the passage. Use the diagrams to help you fill some of the gaps.

catch microscopes fruit seen ants swimming tongue teeth creatures dancing angler mammal hide appearance Africa

Strange Creatures

Modern electron ____________[1] help us to see unusual tiny creatures no one has ever ____________[2] before. Of course, we wouldn't have needed one to see the 330 pound jellyfish, each the size of a washing machine, ____________[3] off Japan's beaches in 2002!

Special deep-sea submarines have found ____________[4] fish with rows of long sharp ____________[5] and their own shining fishing rod to ____________[6] prey. A lizard in the Namib Desert in ____________[7] hops from leg to leg on hot sand and looks as though it is ____________[8].

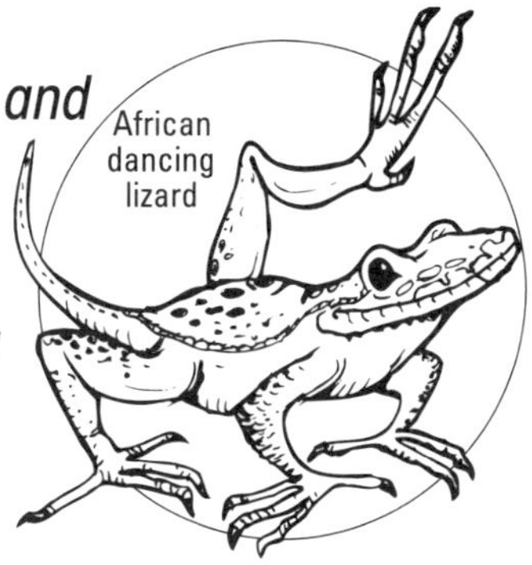

The odd-looking African aardvark eats ____________[9] and termites and sometimes smells like rotten ____________[10], which attracts these insects. The chameleon, a lizard with a ____________[11] as long as its body, changes color to ____________[12] from its enemies or sneak up on insects. The Australian platypus is a ____________[13] which lays eggs, and when scientists first heard reports about its strange ____________[14] they didn't believe such weird ____________[15] existed. How wrong could they be!

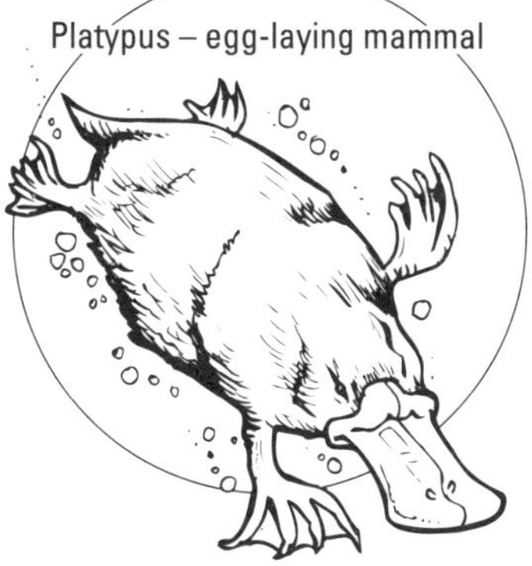

Teacher Information

Animated Films

Objectives

- To introduce to students some background information on animated films so popular with young children.
- To show such films are one of the many forms of communication.
- To throw light on a communication form seen by probably 100% of children in our schools.
- To reinforce the use of verbs in sentences.

Teaching Points

- Discuss the function of verbs and their tenses.
- Discuss the characters students have seen in animated films.
- Show a video (e.g. Shrek, Sinbad). Who were the bad characters? How could you tell? What were the characteristics of the hero?
- What other communication forms do we have?
- Class survey on the most popular animated films seen – graph the results, discuss differences between boys' and girls' choices.
- Discuss terms – storyboard, digital camera, animators, etc.

Evaluation

- Are the students aware of the enormous changes in communication from cave drawings to life-like computer imaging?
- Did students particularly enjoy this topic?
- Are students aware of the many current communication techniques?

Answers

1. began	2. painted	3. complete
4. displayed	5. records	6. placed
7. move	8. jump	9. checks
10. gallops	11. use	12. drawn
13. mixed	14. take	15. paid

Use the following VERBS to complete the passage.

painted gallops records drawn take displayed checks use complete jump began paid placed mixed move

---

Animated Films

Animation perhaps ______[1] *when our early ancestors drew animals galloping across cave walls or ancient Egyptians* ______[2] *pictures inside tombs and temples.*

To produce an animated cartoon, teams of artists ______[3] *dozens of drawings which are then* ______[4] *on a "storyboard." A digital camera linked to a computer* ______[5] *them in the story's correct order. For recording, each drawing is* ______[6] *under a sheet of glass to keep it flat and absolutely still. If the drawings* ______[7] *slightly, the film's characters will* ______[8] *around jerkily on the screen. The computer then* ______[9] *each moving sequence of drawings to see that a horse* ______[10] *correctly or a hero's walking action looks natural.*

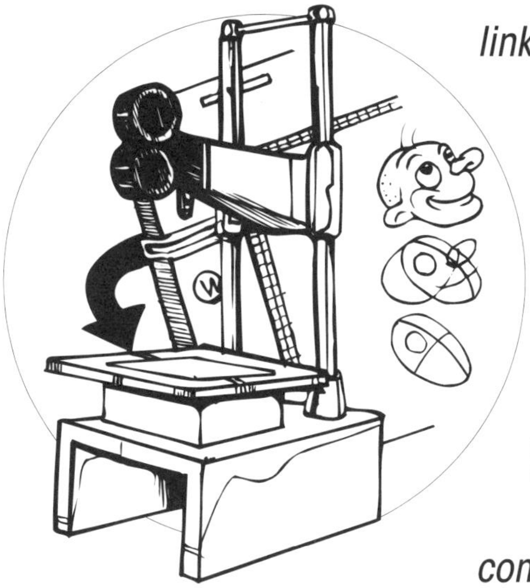

In recent years, some artists have preferred to ______[11] *human characters instead of the cartoon animals* ______[12] *by Walt Disney's "animators." Recent films like* Stuart Little *have* ______[13] *real-life actors and computer-animated characters which almost look real. It is thought that, in future, computer animations more life-like than Stuart Little may* ______[14] *some screen roles from real actors to avoid the huge salaries* ______[15] *to film stars.*

Teacher Information

Children's Toys

Objectives

- To use a cloze exercise on a topic that students are familiar with.
- To point out that all toys are not safe and care needs to be taken, especially with young children.
- To show how toys have become much more sophisticated compared with those used by Greek/Roman children.

Teaching Points

- Point out how ancient children found pleasure in the simplest of toys like tops, hoops, dolls, etc. (as do modern children).
- Students to bring in toy packages to discuss the warnings on them.
- Discuss safety standards in countries which export toys to this country.
- Student class talks on their favorite toy.
- Students to research the most popular toys in a number of countries around the world.
- Small groups trace the history of a chosen toy (e.g. top, yo–yo, hoop, doll) and report to the class.

Evaluation

- Was the particular topic enjoyed by the students?
- Do the students realize how the types of toys and their complexity has changed over the centuries?
- Are the students aware of the dangers some toys present to their younger siblings?
- Were the student talks informative/enjoyable?
- Did each small group cooperate well to seek research information?

Answers

1. kites	2. today	3. Christmas
4. spinning	5. purchased	6. dangers
7. dangerous	8. swallowed	9. injury
10. countries	11. film	12. young
13. cartwheels	14. ignore	15. batteries

Use the following words to complete the passage.

young dangerous spinning countries dangers today ignore swallowed purchased Christmas injury cartwheels kites film batteries

---

Children's Toys

Ancient Greek and Roman children flew their ______ 1, rolled hoops, and spun tops, but didn't have the variety of toys you have ______ 2.

Many very expensive toys appear around ______ 3. ______ 4 tops are still very popular toys and can be ______ 5 for as little as $15.

Toys are great fun but there are also ______ 6. Messages on some packages warn that a particular toy may be ______ 7 for children under three as it contains tiny parts which could be ______ 8. Others may have sharp points which could cause ______ 9 or contain poisonous liquids, such as are sometimes found in paints or crayons. We must remember that some ______ 10 which make toys do not have our strict safety standards. One toy, a plastic elf based on a character in a Harry Potter ______ 11, has been described as very dangerous for ______ 12 children.

Some modern toys are amazing—they can do ______ 13, talk to you, and remind you they are there when you ______ 14 them! There are plastic balls with ______ 15 inside which even bounce around by themselves!

Teacher Information

Graffiti

Objectives

- To illustrate that graffiti tags deface public/private property and are considered to be irresponsible by the general community.
- To show that responsible, approved graffiti is an admired art form.
- To show that graffiti is a form of communication for street gangs/individuals.
- To introduce the students to rhyming couplets in a poem format.

Teaching Points

- Discuss the efforts to combat graffiti – local councils employing graffiti-removal teams, anti-graffiti paint, increased fines, etc.
- Discuss the dilemma students might have reporting their "tagger" friends to the police.
- Challenge students to find what language the word graffiti comes from and what the singular noun is (graffito).
- Elicit suggestions from the class to combat the problem. (Some of the world's most beautiful cities have this problem.)
- Discuss terms from the passage – "chemical blasts," "visual pollution," "marks their territory," "bubble letter," etc.

Evaluation

- Did the topic engender more enthusiasm than usual?
- Were there sensible, informed suggestions from the students who opposed/supported steps to combat the problem?
- Did the rhyming words in couplets make it easier to fill the gaps?
- Did students realize graffiti is a from of communication from groups/individuals to others in the community?

Answers

1. walls	2. scrawls	3. right	4. site
5. mine	6. sign	7. trains	8. brain
9. know	10. show	11. town	12. down
13. display	14. way	15. adults	16. results

Use the following words to complete the poem. Use the rhyming words to help you fill in the spaces.

site know results display sign walls brains town
mine adults right trains show way down scrawls

Graffiti

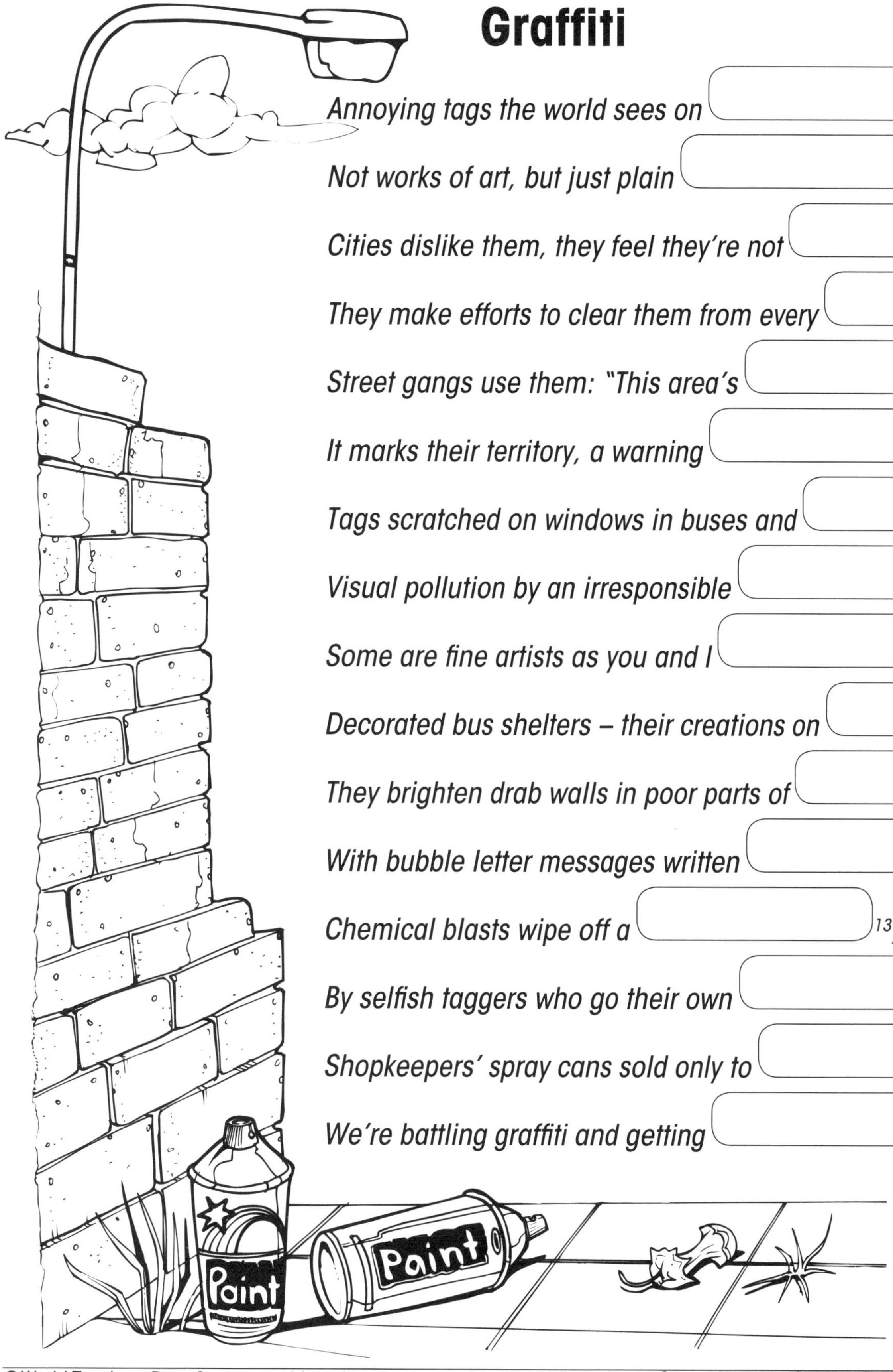

Annoying tags the world sees on ________ [1],
Not works of art, but just plain ________ [2].
Cities dislike them, they feel they're not ________ [3],
They make efforts to clear them from every ________ [4].
Street gangs use them: "This area's ________ [5],"
It marks their territory, a warning ________ [6].
Tags scratched on windows in buses and ________ [7],
Visual pollution by an irresponsible ________ [8].
Some are fine artists as you and I ________ [9],
Decorated bus shelters – their creations on ________ [10].
They brighten drab walls in poor parts of ________ [11],
With bubble letter messages written ________ [12].
Chemical blasts wipe off a ________ [13],
By selfish taggers who go their own ________ [14].
Shopkeepers' spray cans sold only to ________ [15],
We're battling graffiti and getting ________ [16].

Teacher Information

Dinosaurs

Objectives

- To develop reading skills using a cloze exercise on a topic popular with school students.
- To show dinosaur fossils are constantly being discovered.
- To add current information to a very popular topic.
- To show that scientists are still seeking the reason why dinosaurs disappeared from the earth.

Teaching Points

- Discuss the meaning of "carnivorous" and "herbivorous."
- Explain terms used in the passage – "predators," "fossils," "expedition."
- Use atlases/classroom maps to locate the countries/regions mentioned in the passage.
- See if any students can research one of the theories explaining why it is thought dinosaurs were wiped out 65 million years ago.
- Have the class collect pictures/photocopies of the many types of dinosaurs, large and small, for a classroom display.
- Have students find the meaning of the word "dinosaur" (from the Greek "deinos" meaning "terrible" and "sauros" meaning "lizard").

Evaluation

- Do the students know the meaning of the vocabulary used?
- Were the students able to find any theories on the extinction of the dinosaurs?
- Can students locate any of the fossil countries/regions on a map?
- Were there sufficient pictures of dinosaurs for the planned display?

Answers

1. size	2. elephant	3. scientists
4. every	5. plains	6. century
7. million	8. found	9. foothills
10. skeleton	11. dinosaur	12. fossils
13. hunted	14. mystery	15. unsolved

Use the following words to complete the passage.

fossils **size** **found** **dinosaur** **mystery** **century** **elephant** **skeleton**
hunted **foothills** **scientists** **unsolved** **million** **plains** **every**

Dinosaurs

Dinosaurs were amazing creatures. Some were plant-eaters while others were meat-eaters. Some were the __________[1] of a chicken! Others were many times bigger than an __________[2] but with a brain the same size as your pet cat's! They lived millions of years ago, but __________[3] discover several new kinds of dinosaur fossil __________[4] year. Discoveries are mainly made in China, Mongolia, the central __________[5] of the U.S., Argentina, and Australia.

At the start of this __________[6], two fossils were discovered in China. They were about 130 __________[7] years old. One is the first to be __________[8] with its feather-like body covering still intact.

Recently, researchers in the __________[9] of the Andes Mountains found the almost complete __________[10] of a meat-eater. It is possibly the world's oldest __________[11] fossil—230 million years old! (It would take you 11 days to count to one million!) The same expedition also found __________[12] of two predators near a river. They had a bird-like skull and __________[13] their prey standing upright on two hind legs.

We know a lot about them—but the __________[14] of why dinosaurs disappeared still remains __________[15].

Teacher Information

Homes of the Future

Objectives

- To develop reading skills through a cloze exercise with a letter format.
- To show students the amazing technological advances they should see in their homes when they are adults.
- To compare modern homes with traditional dwellings built by American Indians, etc.
- To use a topic which will affect all class members.

Teaching Points

- Discuss the wide variety of building materials used over the centuries.
- Locate the regions in far North America where the Inuit people live.
- Show illustrations of homes once used – tepees, igloos, etc.
- Point out how many early homes were built of materials found in the environment (timber, animals hides, ice, etc.), whereas many future homes will include features developed through scientific progress.

Evaluation

- How interesting was the topic to the students?
- To show that these changes are already being introduced - do any students watch a plasma TV screen at home?
- Do students fully understand the ideas in the passage or do they require further explanation?

Answers

1. kinds	2. animal	3. future
4. screens	5. walls	6. wood
7. change	8. darkens	9. clear
10. panes	11. outside	12. most
13. skin	14. thumbprint	15. boring

Use the following words to complete the passage.

clear	**screens**	**thumbprint**	**animal**	**wood**	**boring**	**skin**	**change**
darkens	**most**	**kinds**	**future**	**walls**	**outside**	**panes**	

Class 4H

Homes of the Future

Mt. Hawke Elementary School

Dear Stephanie,

In your letter you mentioned what you are studying at school. We're studying different ________[1] of homes—mud-brick houses, tepees made from ________[2] hides, Inuit igloos built of ice, and American pioneer cabins. But our teacher says the homes of the ________[3] will amaze us all!

We've all heard about huge plasma TV ________[4] we'll have hanging on the ________[5], but what about walls made from soy flour and recycled newspaper! This is a product called "Environ" which looks like granite but can be drilled, hammered, and sawed like ________[6]. And there's a paint being developed for outside walls that can ________[7] color! When the weather is cold the paint ________[8] to absorb more heat. (Remember that T-shirt you had that changed color when you got hot?)

How about windows that go ________[9] at the flick of a switch! "Viracon" uses liquid crystals (the stuff used in watch screens), sandwiching them between ________[10] of glass to make it look foggy. When electricity is passed through, the liquid crystals go clear and, hey presto, you can see ________[11]! Amazing!

But that's not the ________[12] amazing thing Mr. Harris said. We'll have a mirror with a camera and LCD screen that can check our health by analyzing ________[13] color! Electronic diaries that will scan a ________[14] to open doors to cars and homes seemed ________[15] after this!

Kate

Teacher Information

Patterns and Numbers in Nature

Objectives

- To develop reading skills through a cloze exercise based on a subject popular with students.
- To reinforce the students' knowledge of nouns.
- To introduce students to interesting, unusual information about the animal world.

Teaching Points

- Reinforce the concept of nouns as naming words, and elicit examples from the class.
- Ask students to name any patterns they see in their environment (e.g. zebra stripes, windows in a skyscraper, brick paving, etc.)
- Explain the terms "hexagonal," "rhomboid," "symmetry," "parallel," "horizontal," etc. used in the passage.
- Ask students to suggest any patterns they can see in nature (e.g. fish scales, a dalmation's spots, cat's whiskers balanced on either side of its mouth, etc.)

Evaluation

- Do students understand the function of nouns in sentences?
- Were the students able to name any patterns in nature/their environment?
- Did students understand the statement that "amoeba know their numbers because they multiply by dividing"?
- Did students enjoy the exercise and perform well?

Answers

1. Patterns	2. hive	3. snowflake
4. butterfly	5. tigers	6. leopards
7. scientists	8. angelfish	9. stripes
10. cockroach	11. legs	12. speeds
13. ground	14. animals	15. numbers

Use the following NOUNS to complete the passage.

angelfish hive legs tigers cockroach Patterns leopards ground snowflake animals stripes butterfly numbers scientists speeds

Patterns and Numbers in Nature

_______[1] are found everywhere in nature. We have the pattern of hexagonal shapes on a honeycomb in a bees' _______[2] and the rhomboid shapes on a snake's scales. There is also the six-sided rotation symmetry of an icy _______[3]. Left and right symmetry is common. The right wing of a beautiful _______[4] is the mirror image of the left one and other insects are the same.

Parallel stripes are seen on _______[5] and zebras but jaguars, cheetahs, and _______[6] have spots. Fish also have stripes and Japanese _______[7] have shown that horizontal stripe patterns on the tropical _______[8] break apart and then rejoin. New _______[9] develop as the fish grows.

Numbers are found too. When a _______[10] moves fast it uses two sets of three legs. The front and back left _______[11] move with the middle right leg and vice versa. When centipedes travel at high _______[12] sometimes only three legs out of 40 touch the _______[13] at one time! Amoeba, tiny _______[14] with only one cell, certainly know their _______[15]. They multiply by dividing!

Teacher Information

Speed!

Objectives

- To develop reading skills through a cloze exercise based on a popular topic.
- To reinforce the students' knowledge of nouns.
- To use an exercise popular with students and a topic frequently discussed in the media.

Teaching Points

- Discuss the advantages/disadvantages of living life at a more leisurely pace.
- Reinforce the concept of nouns as naming words and elicit examples from the class.
- Read out other examples of odd speed records from the *Guiness Book Of Records.*
- Discuss the value of seatbelts when traveling at high speeds.
- See if any students can beat the record time by Japanese school students in a 50–meter, three-legged race.
- List four necessary safety features required for a bicycle/its student rider if traveling at high speeds.

Evaluation

- Do the students understand the function of nouns in a sentence?
- Were students enthusiastic about the three–legged race?
- Did the students participate well in the discussion periods of the lesson?

Answers

1. grandparents	2. people	3. road
4. destination	5. hour	6. cars
7. towns	8. records	9. run
10. miles	11. sausages	12. friends
13. seconds	14. race	15. school

Use the following NOUNS to complete the passage.

cars run friends grandparents miles records race roads sausages people school towns hour seconds destination

Speed!

Your ______[1] probably tell you that life is just too fast for them today. They think too many ______[2] want to live their lives at breakneck speed. High-speed ______[3] have been built all around the world so people can reach their ______[4] more quickly at speeds of at least 60 miles per ______[5]. That's much faster than the early steam ______[6] in Britain. They could only travel at 2 miles per hour in ______[7] because of a law passed in 1865. It was quicker to walk!

And what about some of the speed ______[8] listed in the 2003 Guinness Book of Records*? They include the fastest backwards ______[9] from Los Angeles to New York—a distance of 1491.3 ______[10]! Another entry tells us that a New Zealander ate eight ______[11] in just one minute. Perhaps you and one of your ______[12] could beat the book's listed record of nine ______[13] for a 50-meter, three-legged ______[14] achieved by the students of a Japanese ______[15]. It's worth a try!*

Teacher Information

Games Around the World

Objectives

- To develop reading skills through a cloze exercise on a topic students should enjoy.
- To give students information on games played by their counterparts from different cultures around the world.
- To give students the experience of providing their own words to fill the gaps.

Teaching Points

- Following the completion of the sheet, have a follow-up lesson where small groups of children rotate around some of the games described in the exercise.
- Explain that there could be a choice of several words when the students select their own.
- Half a box from a supermarket could be used for the "Haba Gaba" game.
- Discuss some of the toys used in ancient Roman/Egyptian times – hoops, dolls, toy chariots, etc.
- Locate on a class map – Nigeria, Holland, Dominican Republic, Sierra Leone, and Inuit regions (N. Canada).

Evaluation

- Were the students aware that many children in poorer countries don't have sophisticated mechanical toys in their games but use simple objects – twigs, stones, coconut shells, etc?
- Did students see any resemblance to the games they play?
- Which game was the most popular? Why?

Answers

1. games	2. Moteca	3. buttons
4. circle	5. round	6. canoe
7. pole	8. guide	9. Africa
10. four	11. stone	12. attempt/try
13. wins	14. eggs	15. last

Use clues from the diagrams and some of your own words to complete the passage.

Games Around the World

For thousands of years many of the world's children have played ________[1] which help to improve their physical and mental skills.

Children in the Dominican Republic play "________[2]" and use a spinning top to try to knock ________[3] off small stones. The stones are placed in a ________[4] drawn on the ground. Inuit children spin a top inside their home and try to run ________[5] the house before it stops spinning!

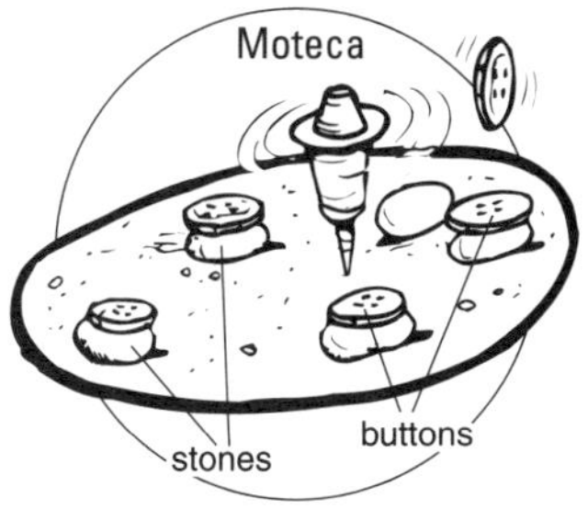

Nigerian youngsters play a war ________[6] game. Team members sit on a ________[7] and move backwards across a "river" drawn on the ground. A ________[8] steers them around obstacles representing rocks, crocodiles, etc.

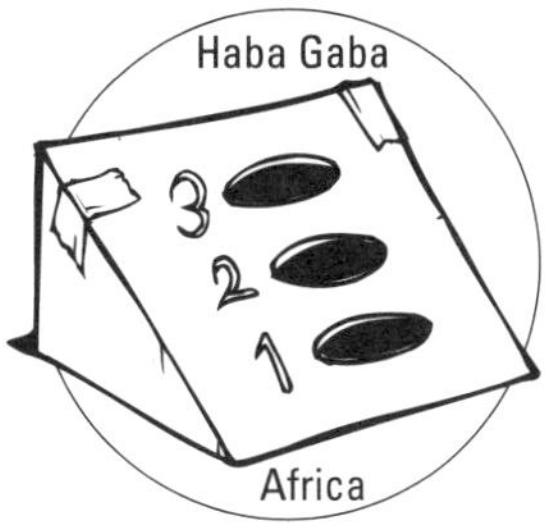

"Haba Gaba" is a game played in Sierra Leone in ________[9], with each player given three throws and the highest score winning.

"Papago" is a native American Indian game using ________[10] paper cups. They are filled with sand. One has a ________[11] hidden in it. If player 1 finds it at his/her first ________[12], he/she earns four points. His/Her second try earns three points and so on. The first player to reach 10 points ________[13] the game.

At Easter, Dutch children gently bump hard-boiled ________[14] together. The person whose egg is the ________[15] to crack is the winner!

Teacher Information

Fighting Malaria

Objectives

- To develop reading skills using a cloze exercise on an important topic of concern to world governments.
- To give students practice in gleaning information from a map/graph in order to find answers.
- To show how much suffering this disease causes around the world.
- To make students aware that precautions must be taken against mosquitos, which spread a variety of diseases.

Teaching Points

- Discuss how one reads the graph numbers on the horizontal axis.
- Give a brief outline of other diseases caused by mosquitoes – yellow fever, etc.
- List ways of avoiding mosquito bites – burning coils, suitable clothing, repellents, etc.
- Explain the terms "resistance," "humid," "genes."
- Emphasize that the dangerous diseases are not such a threat in the cooler regions of North America.

Evaluation

- Did students find difficulty reading the graph?
- Were students able to gain information from the map?
- Are students not worried about their chances of contracting malaria?
- Are they aware that millions of children in tropical regions of the world do not have satisfactory health services to protect them?

Answers

1. warm	2. bite	3. children
4. disease	5. drugs	6. century
7. scientists	8. harmless	9. northern
10. Russia	11. Africa	12. year
13. Australia	14. four	15. Korea

Use the following words to complete the passage. Look at the map and bar graph to fill some spaces.

northern **warm** **Russia** **four** **children** **bite** **harmless** **year**
century **disease** **Australia** **Africa** **drugs** **Korea** **scientists**

Fighting Malaria

Malaria is a disease found in ____________ [1] humid climates. It is spread by a ____________ [2] from the female Anopheles mosquito. Millions of people die each year; most are ____________ [3] under the age of 10.

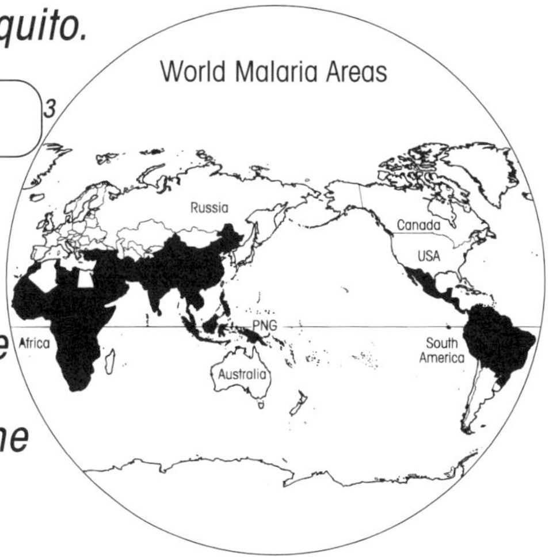

Control of the ____________ [4] has become more difficult as it has developed a resistance to some of the ____________ [5] used by doctors.

However, in the 21st ____________ [6] experts expect to find a cure. In 2002, ____________ [7] discovered the mosquito's gene pattern. They now hope to make the insect ____________ [8] by experimenting with those genes.

Malaria Cases: Asia-Pacific Region: 2000

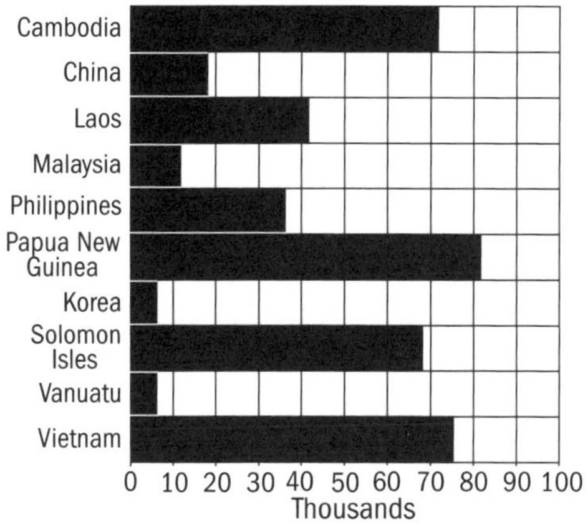

In the ____________ [9] hemisphere, America, Canada, and ____________ [10] are free of malaria, but people in ____________ [11], India, and South America suffer a great deal. The graph of the Asia-Pacific region shows most cases in the ____________ [12] 2000 were found in Papua New Guinea, which lies just north of ____________ [13]. Of the countries listed, only ____________ [14] had fewer than 20,000 cases, and ____________ [15] had about the same number as Vanuatu.

Teacher Information

Nature Fights Back

Objectives

- To develop reading skills using a cloze exercise on the interesting topic of animal/insect pests.
- To encourage the search for meaning by omitting various parts of speech.
- To give students information on animal/insect pests and the problems they bring.

Teaching Points

- Ask students to name creatures they regard as pests. Why?
- Discuss the meaning of the title. (Refers to the years of destruction of animal habitats, extinction of species, etc. So nature is fighting back.)
- On a class map, locate the various countries of regions named in the exercise.
- Discuss which creature the students regard as the greatest threat. Why is this?
- Suggest the students fill in the gaps they are absolutely sure of first.
- Have students do some research in their own time and report to the class one interesting fact about any of the creatures in the exercise.

Evaluation

- Did the students find the topic interesting?
- Did the students find any difficulty selecting the correct answers?
- Was there a good response to doing research in their own time?
- Was this nature topic one the students could relate to easily?

Answers

1. hunt	2. getting	3. sugar
4. lay	5. tadpoles	6. poisoned
7. spread	8. painful	9. dollars
10. farmers	11. South	12. damage
13. foxes	14. suburbs	15. destroying

Use the following words to complete the passage.

dollars   tadpoles   getting   South   hunt   spread   foxes   lay
painful   suburbs   farmers   poisoned   sugar   destroying   damage

---

Nature Fights Back

Many animals are endangered or extinct because we __________[1] them or destroy their environment. Perhaps now they're __________[2] their own back!

Cane toads were brought to Queensland in Australia to control __________[3] cane beetles. They've increased to huge numbers as they can __________[4] up to 10,000 eggs at a time. They are spreading across north Australia, eating native __________[5] and lizards and pets can be __________[6] if they eat these toads!

This century, South American fire ants have __________[7] northwards across some states in the U.S. They have a __________[8] bite and cost America millions of __________[9] each year. Their nest mounds are so hard they damage farm machinery, so __________[10] are very unhappy.

Argentine ants, also from __________[11] America, were recently found in New Zealand. They __________[12] fruit crops and climb trees, sometimes killing baby native birds.

Bears in Canada and __________[13] in Britain are often found scavenging food from trash cans in city __________[14]. Thousands of crown-of-thorns starfish are slowly __________[15] some of the world's finest reefs. Looks like nature's fighting back!

Teacher Information

Space Travel

Objectives

- To develop reading skills using a cloze exercise on a topic both current and interesting.
- To reinforce the understanding of the work of adjectives in sentences.
- To introduce students to the remarkable scientific advances which make space travel possible.

Teaching Points

- Discuss the work of adjectives in sentences.
- Explain that adjectives usually come immediately before the noun they describe but can appear anywhere in the sentence.
- Discuss any unfamiliar terms used – "orbiting," "fascinated," "decade," "shuttle," "mission."
- Conduct a class discussion on why explorers want to explore unknown territory (e.g. Amundsen at the South Pole, Marco Polo in China, Livingstone in the jungles of Africa, etc.).
- Discuss briefly the development of aircraft from the Wright Brothers to jet planes to rocket ships.

Evaluation

- Was interest in the topic sufficient to lead to mini-group/individual projects on famous explorers?
- Were girls as interested in the topic as boys?
- Do students fully understand the work of adjectives as descriptive words which add to the quality of sentences?

Answers

1. brilliant	2. important	3. red
4. special	5. far–off	6. outer
7. valuable	8. regular	9. thrilling
10. different	11. harmful	12. several
13. enormous	14. new	15. reusable

Use the following ADJECTIVES to complete the passage.

harmful valuable special enormous reusable several red brilliant thrilling outer new important far-off regular different

Space Travel

Space travel has fascinated the world's ________[1] scientists for years. Since the moon landings, the ________[2] targets have been Venus and the "________[3] planet," Mars—which are both closer to Earth than the other planets.

A ________[4] camera on the "Odyssey" spacecraft has been photographing the surface of Mars and the "Cassini" probe will orbit ________[5] Saturn in the near future. The "Stardust" spacecraft is at present collecting dust from a comet's tail in ________[6] space and will return ________[7] information to Earth several years from now.

Rocket planes can fly over 4,000 m/h and ________[8] space flights are expected during the 21st century. The price of one ticket on "Xerus," a rocket plane planned to take tourists on a ________[9] one-hour trial flight in the next decade, is $130,000!

Astronauts from ________[10] countries have spent months orbiting in space to test possible ________[11] effects. These experiments will lead to space stations where people will live and work for ________[12] years.

If space travel for ordinary people is to become a reality, the scientists need to cut the ________[13] costs. At present, a shuttle's main fuel tank drops away in flight and must be replaced for each ________[14] mission. One way to reduce this huge expense is to develop ________[15] launch vehicles, and various designs are being tested.

Teacher Information

Our Changing Language

Objectives

- To develop reading skills using a cloze exercise familiar to students.
- To show how our language is always changing.
- To give examples of changes students/adults are presently using.

Teaching Points

- Give examples of changes parents/grandparents have become accustomed to – telephone to phone, omnibus to bus, refrigerator to fridge, etc.
- Discuss a recent change – text messaging, e.g. URL8 for "you are late," etc.
- Discuss word meanings young people change – "wicked" means "good" rather than "evil." Elicit from the students other similar changes; e.g. "cool," "gross," etc.
- Explain how the English language has been constantly altered over the centuries by assimilating words from other nations through trade, conquest, or social interactions; e.g. Anglo-Saxons, French, Roman (Latin), Germanic tribes, American Indians, Spanish, etc.
- Students work in small groups to compile lists of words which have changed. e.g. air to plane; television to TV.
- Students to send their own text message to a classmate.

Evaluation

- Were the student groups successful in compiling their word list?
- Could the compiling of word changes be a continuing/activity throughout the year?
- Did the students enjoy the exercise?
- Do the students realize our language has been changing throughout the centuries and will continue to do so?

Answers

1. centuries	2. word	3. England
4. called	5. different	6. lazy
7. plane	8. years	9. Roman
10. shorten	11. nite	12. changing
13. something	14. adults	15. students

Use the following words to complete the passage.

something lazy England changing called adults centuries
years plane different word nite shorten students Roman

Our Changing Language

There are thousands of languages and over the ______ [1] our English language has seen many changes. An Old English ______ [2] like "cese" has become "cheese" and "forca" is now "fork." The Saxon invaders of ______ [3] called short garments "shirts," whereas the Danes, also invaders, ______ [4] them "skirts." Now, centuries later, they mean totally ______ [5] articles of clothing!

Humans tend to be ______ [6] so refrigerator, omnibus, airplane and telephone have become fridge, bus, ______ [7] and phone. Even Shakespeare shortened "do not" to "don't"—and that was over 300 ______ [8] ago! Our words "autumn" and "hymn" were once ancient ______ [9] words "autumnus" and "hymnus" but, hey, let's ______ [10] them!

Mobile phone use has also shortened our written word - gr8 – "great"; ______ [11] "night."

Nowadays, young people are ______ [12] our language. Who'd have thought that ______ [13] you did that was "wicked" was good! A wicked witch—a good one? "Gross" can mean 144 items to ______ [14], but "yuck" to their children. Let's hope the ______ [15] reading this think it's "cool"!

Teacher Information

Computers and Your Health

Objectives

- To develop reading skills using a cloze exercise on a topic familiar to all students.
- To reinforce the students' knowledge of adjectives.
- To show the potential health risks of spending too many hours in front of a computer screen.

Teaching Points

- Discuss the important cautionary measures to be taken when using computers.
- Discuss the work of adjectives in sentences and elicit examples from the students.
- Point out that adjectives can appear in front of or after the noun they relate to.
- Complete a class graph on how many hours each student uses a computer (a) at school (b) at home.
- Check children are acting on the advice given in the exercise.

Evaluation

- How did the students fare on a different exercise to pick out adjectives?
- Are students practicing good habits during computer lessons?
- Do students report any ill–effects they might experience?

Answers

1. English	2. young	3. developing
4. serious	5. America	6. clever
7. suitable	8. Japanese	9. painful
10. unfortunate	11. Long	12. overweight
13. unsuitable	14. comfortable	15. short

Use the following ADJECTIVES to complete the passage.

Japanese young clever overweight serious Long painful short unsuitable English unfortunate comfortable developing America suitable

Computers and Your Health

An ______[1] expert warns that most computers are designed for adults. He says ______[2] children using them can damage their health. A child's ______[3] muscles and bones could be harmed and ______[4] neck and bone problems follow in later life. Recent research in ______[5] and England shows many school students suffer frequent neck and back pain. As a result, ______[6] designers are being asked to design ______[7] computers for children.

______[8] experts have found we shouldn't be staring at computer screens for hour after hour. They reported that ______[9] headaches and eyestrain were problems for those ______[10] or foolish enough to spend over five hours a day in front of a computer. ______[11] periods sitting down are also thought to be one reason we see so many ______[12] children. Another study found many schools had ______[13] chairs and tables which couldn't be raised or lowered for different age groups.

REMEMBER! Position the chair and keyboard so you are ______[14], rest your feet flat on the floor, and take frequent ______[15] breaks.

Teacher Information

Benefits from Space Research

Objectives

- To develop reading skills using a non-fiction exercise on a topic affecting all of us.
- To encourage the search for meaning by omitting only nouns.
- To reinforce the students' knowledge of the function of nouns in sentences.
- To make the students aware that there are many benefits from the billions of dollars spent on space research.

Teaching Points

- Discuss the types of nouns in the exercise (proper, common) and ask the students for examples of nouns. Describe any noun categories which are suggested (e.g. common, proper, collective, abstract).
- Have students collect other examples of research benefits and inform the class in oral reports.
- Discuss why astronauts volunteer for such dangerous missions – search for glory? sense of adventure? prestige? Is the money spent worthwhile?
- Discuss terms used in the exercise – "sensors," "paralyzed," "stimulate," "NASA," "ceramic," "corrosion," "screened," "archeologists."
- Show a "Superman" film with Christopher Reeve and mention the work he did to raise millions of dollars for spinal research – appearances, pressure on governments because of his high profile, etc.

Evaluation

- Can the students recognize nouns?
- Were students active in discussion periods?
- Do students have an opinion on the billions of dollars spent on space research when there are so many problems on Earth (poverty, disease, starving millions, etc.)?

Answers

1. bodies	2. Sweden	3. doctors
4. horse	5. signals	6. pictures
7. children	8. problems	9. metals
10. friction	11. suits	12. pottery
13. dolphins	14. paint	15. Statue

Use the following NOUNS to complete the passage.

horse pottery pictures doctors suits Statue bodies signals metals dolphins friction Sweden problems paint children

---

Benefits from Space Research

The enormous pressures on astronauts' ________[1] at lift-off led to a new foam material made in ________[2]. It spreads pressure around the body as a person sleeps and now ________[3] recommend mattresses made of it.

"Superman" star, Christopher Reeve, was paralyzed when he fell from a ________[4]. He used a space research invention which sends tiny electrical ________[5] to stimulate muscles and nerves and maintain his fitness.

Christopher Reeve

NASA technology, which took amazing ________[6] of the moon, is now used for eye testing. Young ________[7] don't sit still long enough for normal tests but now thousands are screened to detect possible future ________[8].

Insulating materials made from ________[9] and ceramics protected the space shuttles from the fierce heat caused by ________[10] as they re-entered Earth's atmosphere. These materials are now used in firefighters' ________[11].

Space research has led to many benefits: sensors which help archaeologists to find ancient ________[12] buried underground and "bleepers" attached to underwater nets to prevent ________[13] from becoming entangled. A ceramic ________[14] used to protect the Apollo launching pad now protects bridges and the ________[15] of Liberty from corrosion!

Teacher Information

The Book or the Film?

Objectives

- To give students practice in using their own words to provide answers.
- To show students that many films they see are derived from popular books from the world's literature.
- To show that both films and books expand our knowledge of literature – its characters, interesting storylines, and so on.

Teaching Points

- Point out that only one word can be used to fill each gap.
- Discuss opinions about books students have read compared to the films made from them.
- Select a book to be read by the class and then view a video based on the book. Were the main characters the same? Was the storyline altered? Were the film characters as you pictured them in your mind after reading the book? Did you prefer the book? Why?
- Which students would rather read the book first? Why?
- Artwork – have students create a poster advertising a book or a film.
- Students list the main characters in books they have read then list the actors they would cast to play those parts and give their reason why.
- Have students make books for a younger class group – complete with simple text and illustrations and based on popular books.

Evaluation

- Did the students participate well in discussion periods?
- Did the majority prefer the book or the film?
- Did they appreciate film is another way of telling stories?
- Were students successful in providing simple and suitable texts in compiling their books for younger children?

Answers

1. wrote	2. film/movie	3. all
4. films/movies	5. read	6. details/parts
7. girl	8. left	9. readers/children
10. before	11. first	12. visualize/imagine/picture
13. minds/heads	14. books	15. library

The Book or the Film?

Would Hans Christian Andersen, who __________[1] The Little Mermaid *around 1836, like the Walt Disney* __________[2] *better than his book? Perhaps he would, with* __________[3] *the wonderful computer images used in modern* __________[4]*!*

Some children prefer the book as they can __________[5] *it at their own speed. Others are disappointed when so many* __________[6] *of the story are omitted by film makers. One* __________[7] *in a recent survey was very annoyed when she found details about a troll and a trapdoor had been* __________[8] *out of a Harry Potter film. Many young* __________[9] *preferred to read the book* __________[10] *they saw the film. They thought that watching the film* __________[11] *took away some of the interest and excitement. A number of children liked to* __________[12] *the various characters in their* __________[13] *using the more detailed descriptions usually found in* __________[14]*. And it costs you absolutely nothing to borrow a book from a public* __________[15]*.*

Which do you prefer?

Teacher Information

Endangered Animal Snippets

Objectives

- To develop reading skills using a cloze exercise on an important topic.
- To give students experience in gleaning information from a map to complete the answers.
- To show students we need to do something to protect endangered species.

Teaching Points

- Discuss some reasons why species are threatened – habitat destroyed by encroaching developments; hunted for ivory, furs, popular food for people; seen as threat to domestic animals, etc.
- Discuss suggestions from students about methods of protecting animals; e.g. laws banning ivory sales or fur coats, etc.
- Point out that information from the map is needed to fill some of the gaps.
- Students each select a threatened animal to design a poster and slogan (e.g. "Save the Bears") – entry fee, the money raised to go to an animal cause.

Evaluation

- Do the students show real concern for the threatened animals?
- Are students enthusiastic about raising money for animal causes?
- Were students successful in gaining the essential information from the map?

Answers

1. protect	2. Santiago	3. elephants
4. medicines	5. skins	6. Madrid
7. find	8. breeding	9. underground
10. Kenya	11. Java	12. diseases
13. Bwindi	14. China	15. surface

Use the following words to complete the passage. Look at the map to fill some of the spaces.

skins protect Bwindi surface find Santiago underground China breeding elephants medicines Kenya Java diseases Madrid

---

Endangered Animal Snippets

An Australian wildlife conservation group was formed in 2001 to __________[1] 50 endangered native mammals. In November 2002, officials from 160 countries met in __________[2], Chile's capital, to discuss trade in endangered species. Outside, hundreds of students protested that __________[3] would suffer if ivory trading bans were lifted.

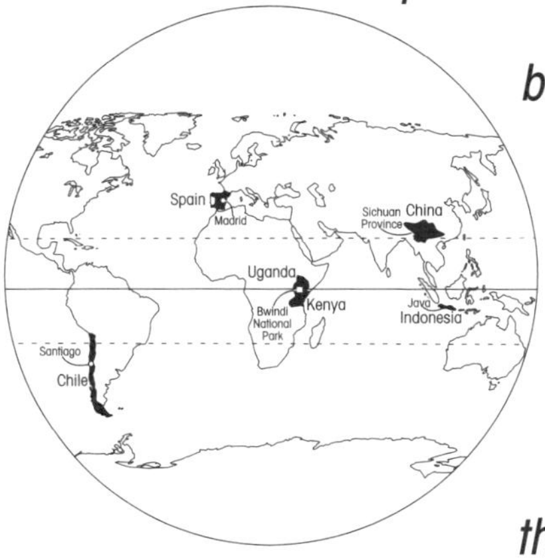

In Asia, "jinbou" is the ancient belief that __________[4] made from animal parts improve poor health. One result is that tiger __________[5] in homes are more common than tigers in the wild! In 2002, in __________[6], Spain's capital, the city's zoo was trying to __________[7] a mate for its Iberian lynx. With fewer than 200 left, they hope to start a __________[8] program. There are fewer than 100 of the world's only __________[9] elephants who move into caves at night in __________[10], Africa. The silvery gibbons native to the island of __________[11] in Indonesia are seriously threatened. Concerned scientists fear that human __________[12] from tourists may reduce mountain gorilla numbers in Uganda's __________[13] National Park. And the number of pandas in a nature reserve in Sichuan province in __________[14] is declining.

Only 5% of the Earth's __________[15] is protected for wildlife. Let's hope that this area is greatly expanded in the 21st century.

Teacher Information

The Water Cycle

Objectives

- To develop reading skills using a cloze exercise on a topic which affects all students.
- To give information on how rainwater goes through different processes before it comes out of our faucets.
- To teach students to glean all the required information from a diagram.

Teaching Points

- Go briefly through the numbered stages in the diagram.
- Discuss terms like "water vapor," "evaporate," "droplets" and what happens in the water treatment works (water purified for domestic use) and the sewage treatment plant (sewage from homes/factories is treated).
- Stress the importance of clean water to drink/return to rivers/oceans.
- Show a water patch on a chalkboard – Fan it with a piece of card until it disappears – this is evaporation.

Evaluation

- Do students fully understand the water cycle?
- Do students understand the dangers when untreated sewage is poured into rivers/oceans as happens in poorer nations where there is little money for treatment plants?
- Do the students realize the importance of water, especially in arid regions?

Answers

1. water	2. oceans	3. land
4. river	5. treatment	6. homes
7. drains	8. sewage	9. ocean
10. sun	11. vapor	12. clouds
13. drops	14. rain	15. cycle

The Water Cycle

The ______[1] cycle is part of our daily lives. Clouds produce rain which falls onto land areas, ______[2], lakes, and rivers. Most of the rain which falls on to the ______[3] is evaporated by the sun's heat or flows underground into the Earth's waterways. Water from a ______[4] or lake can be purified in a water ______[5] plant. This clean water is used in factories and ______[6] and then ______[7] carry the waste water from these buildings to a ______[8] treatment plant. Any unused treated water is then returned to the ______[9] and rivers where the cycle begins again.

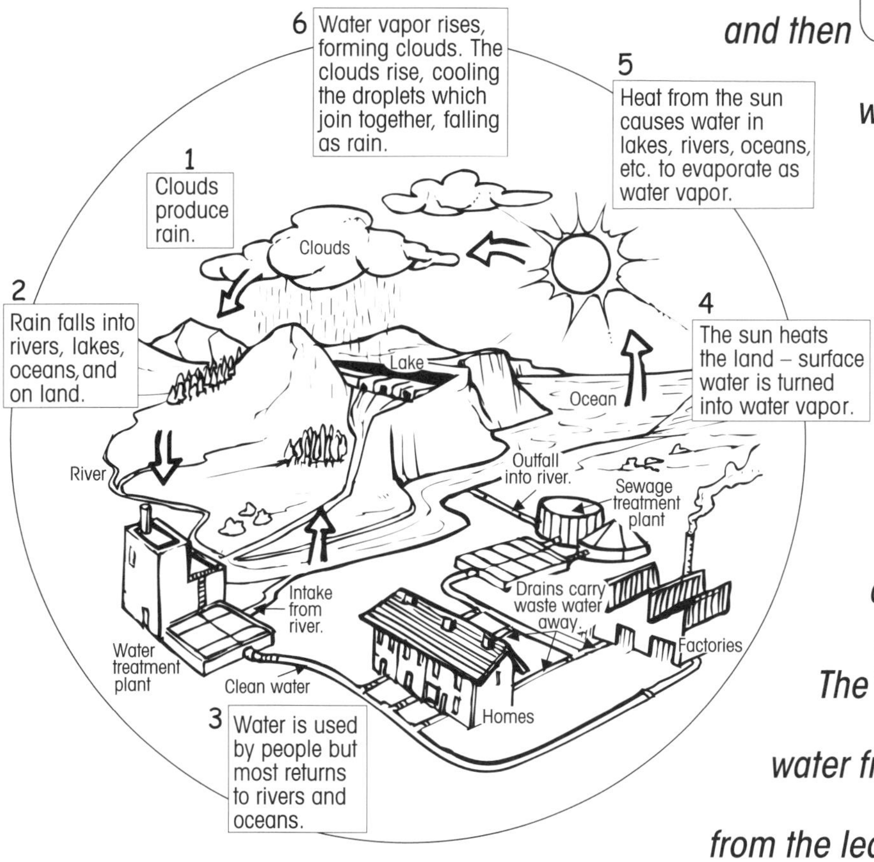

The ______[10] evaporates water from the Earth's surface and from the leaves of plants. This invisible water ______[11] rises and cools into tiny water droplets which form ______[12]. As the clouds rise higher the water vapor cools even more and the drops join together to form bigger drops of water. These ______[13] become too heavy to stay in the air, so they fall as ______[14]. The sun heats the water and the ______[15] begins again.

Teacher Information

Multicultural Foods

Objectives

- To make students aware of some of the benefits immigration brings.
- To introduce students to a variety of exotic dishes.
- To give students experience in gleaning information from an illustration.

Teaching Points

- Discuss the various foods mentioned and find how many students have been to Chinese, Thai, etc. restaurants or had take-out meals from these restaurants.
- Organize parents to give students a "multicultural day" where parents bring samples of food they have cooked (provide them with simple recipes).
- Discuss the proposition that immigrants cook their native foods to maintain touch with their homelands.
- Arrange with a local ethnic cafe/restaurant for a meal with a varied menu. Table manners to be part of the experience.

Evaluation

- Do students realize the importance of familiar foods to immigrants far from their homelands?
- Did the students successfully use the diagram to gain information?
- Do students realize how valuable immigrants can be to a country.

Answers

1. millions	2. elsewhere	3. recipes
4. diners	5. French	6. duck
7. lime	8. cashew	9. hot
10. rolls	11. sweet	12. make
13. grandparents	14. enjoy	15. citizens

Use the following words to complete the passage. Use the illustrations to fill one of the spaces.

duck cashew hot French lime citizens sweet make grandparents rolls millions diners recipes enjoy elsewhere

---

Multicultural Foods

For many years, ________[1] of people have moved from their own countries to seek a better life ________[2]. With them they took their traditional ________[3] which they introduced to generations of ________[4] in their new homeland.

We now have restaurants which serve us ________[5] dishes with frogs' legs! Chinese restaurants have their sliced ________[6] with bean sprouts and ginger.

Families around the country eat take-out Thai meals flavored with ________[7] leaves, coconut milk, and ________[8] nuts. Indian migrants have brought spicy meat dishes with delicious ________[9] sauces. Vietnamese vegetarian spring ________[10] dipped in a tasty thin sauce are also very popular with diners. And everyone loves baklava, ________[11] Greek pastries made with honey and nuts!

These exotic foods ________[12] the potatoes, roast meat, and vegetables eaten by your ________[13] sound very ordinary, don't they? I'm sure we all ________[14] these tasty foods brought by our new ________[15].

Teacher Information

The Harry Potter Phenomenon

Objectives

- To develop reading skills using a cloze exercise on a topic popular with school students.
- To reinforce the students' knowledge of the nouns used in the exercise (common, proper).
- To give the students some background information on J.K. Rowling.

Teaching Points

- Discuss the class's favorite characters from the Harry Potter books.
- Elicit from the class examples of common and proper nouns.
- Have children to draw/color a character of their own. Write a sentence about the character and give him/her a name using alliteration (e.g. Silly Susan, Boring Billy etc.) as in the Potter books.
- Conduct a brief teaching board exercise where students sort out common/proper nouns from a list.
- Discuss the term "fantasy world."

Evaluation

- Can the students recognize common and proper nouns?
- Did the students' familiarity with the topic lead to the exercise being well done?
- Was it an enjoyable experience for the class, including those students who hadn't seen the films?

Answers

1. author	2. wizard	3. child
4. Horse	5. Paris	6. Africa
7. books	8. awards	9. languages
10. films	11. names	12. Myrtle
13. schools	14. booksellers	15. truancy

Use the following NOUNS to complete the passage.

awards Horse author Africa wizard films books booksellers Myrtle names languages child truancy schools Paris

The Harry Potter Phenomenon

Joanne Kathleen Rowling is the ______[1] of the popular books about 10-year-old orphan Harry Potter, who is a young ______[2]. The author was born in England and says as a ______[3] she "lived in a fantasy world." Her favorite book, "The Little White ______[4]," influenced the Harry Potter series of seven planned books. Rowling taught English in ______[5], France, for a year and also worked for Amnesty International in ______[6].

Her ______[7] have been praised by reviewers throughout Europe and have won many European book ______[8]. They have been translated into more than 28 ______[9], sold in more than 130 countries and made into ______[10] which are exciting and very, very popular.

Children love the interesting character ______[11] like Helga Hufflepuff, Moaning ______[12] and Nearly Headless Nick. Book sales have been huge but some ______[13] have banned them because of their emphasis on witchcraft. When ______[14] released the third book in Britain, they were asked to sell them after school hours so that ______[15] wouldn't be a problem!

Teacher Information

Antarctica

Objectives

- To develop reading skills using a cloze exercise on a fascinating area of the world.
- To reinforce the skill of gleaning information from graphs.
- To make students aware of the teeming wildlife in such a harsh area of the world.

Teaching Points

- Point out that the region is one of the coldest and windiest areas in the world.
- Research a brief outline of Antarctica explorers – Scott, Amundsen, Shackleton, Mawson – students to research/report orally.
- Plan an exercise to follow a lesson on bar graphs and how to read them along the horizontal axis.
- Discuss the terms "unique," "square mile" (e.g. 1 m x 1 m, 2 m x $^1/_2$ m, etc.).
- Discuss the battle against multinationals who want to develop the region (oil, minerals) which could decimate the animal life (e.g. Exxon Valdez oil spill).

Evaluation

- How well did students use the graph?
- Do students appreciate that one of the last natural regions on Earth must be protected?
- How well did students research information on Antarctic explorers?

Answers

1. windiest	2. minke	3. blue
4. protests	5. preserved	6. southern
7. penguins	8. ships	9. harmful
10. nations	11. oil	12. islands
13. declare	14. largest	15. size

Use the following words to complete the passage. Use information from the graph to fill some spaces.

nations preserved minke islands windiest oil penguins protests size harmful southern declare blue ships largest

---

Antarctica

Antarctica is 5.4 million square miles in area, the coldest and one of the __________[1] regions on Earth. Its waters teem with life like the __________[2] whales, which reach 32.8 feet in feet. This is one-third the size of the __________[3] whale. Unfortunately, whalers killed over 400 minke whales in 2001 despite __________[4] from around the world.

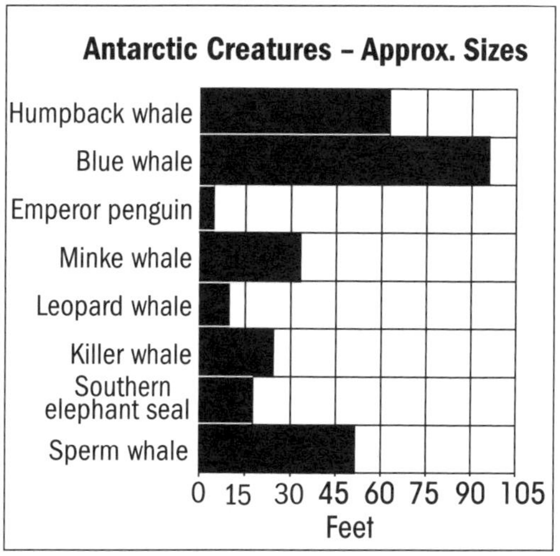

The environmental group Greenpeace believes Antarctica should be __________[5] as a world park. It thinks its wildlife, like leopard seals, the __________[6] elephant seals, and the emperor __________[7], should be protected for future generations. Greenpeace __________[8] regularly visit the region to interfere with whaling fleets or check on possible __________[9] developments in this unique environment. It realizes that several __________[10] are interested in the area as it may hold huge deposits of __________[11] and minerals.

The Australian Heard and McDonald __________[12] form part of the Antarctic region. By early 2003, Australia will __________[13] them part of the world's latest and __________[14] marine park. It will be 16 million acres in area, almost the __________[15] of Switzerland!

Teacher Information

Astronauts

Objectives

- To develop reading skills using a topic popular with and interesting for students.
- To give students practice in using their own words to fill in the gaps.
- To give information on the problems of space travel.

Teaching Points

- Emphasize a word can only be used once and only one word is to be used in each gap.
- More care is needed to read the text around the missing word in order to select a correct answer.
- Explain term "radiation storms" – see teacher's notes.
- Have students research information on Valentina Tereshkova.
- Discuss why people want to be astronauts – sense of adventure? the glory? serving their country?
- Remind students that several correct words could be useful in some gaps.

Evaluation

- Do students appreciate the problems/dangers astronauts face in outer space?
- Are students more successful when able to select their own words to complete the exercise?
- Was a variety of correct words used in some answers, leading to discussion on whether one word was more appropriate than another?

Answers

1. sailed	2. sun	3. lives
4. younger	5. old	6. fit
7. examinations/tests	8. taught/trained	9. problems
10. quarters/areas	11. poor	12. eat
13. future	14. Women	15. first

Select your OWN WORDS to complete the passage. Use a word only once and have one word in each gap.

Astronauts

Explorers have ____[1] on unknown waters, trekked across hot deserts under a burning ____[2],and cut their way through dense jungles. There are also courageous astronauts who risk their ____[3] as they explore outer space. Chinese astronauts have to be ____[4] than 45, but former American astronaut John Glenn, a U.S. senator, was 77 years ____[5] when he last flew in space! The American astronauts have no age limit but need to be very ____[6] to pass extremely strict physical ____[7].

New entrants are ____[8] by top scientists and experienced astronauts who make them aware of the ____[9] they will face in space. These problems include cramped living ____[10], radiation storms, space debris, zero gravity (weightlessness), motion sickness, and ____[11] eye-hand coordination. Astronauts also have to ____[12] freeze-dried food, but experiments to produce an onboard ecosystem by scientists in Germany could see astronauts eating fresh fish in the near ____[13].

____[14] have also taken huge risks in space. Russian cosmonaut Valentina Tereshkova was the ____[15] woman in space and American Eileen Collins the first to command a space shuttle.

Do you have what it takes to be an astronaut in the 21st century?

NOTES